QUESTIONING HISTORY

THE AMERICAN COLONIES

Asking Tough Questions

by Jennifer Kaul

Consultant
Tim Solie
Adjunct Professor of History
Minnesota State University, Mankato
Mankato, Minnesota

CAPSTONE PRESS
a capstone imprint

Capstone Captivate is published by Capstone Press, an imprint of Capstone.
1710 Roe Crest Drive
North Mankato, Minnesota 56003
www.capstonepub.com

Library of Congress Cataloging-in-Publication Data is available on the Library of Congress website.
ISBN: 978-1-4966-8466-0 (library binding)
ISBN: 978-1-4966-8812-5 (paperback)
ISBN: 978-1-4966-8486-8 (eBook PDF)

Summary: Why did the Pilgrims and other settlers come to North America? How did Native nations react to white settlers on their land? How was the landscape changed by the colonists? These questions and others are examined to inspire critical thinking for young readers.

Editorial Credits
Editor: Aaron Sautter; Designer: Sara Radka; Media Researcher: Eric Gohl; Production Specialist: Spencer Rosio

Image Credits
Alamy: Niday Picture Library, 15; Bridgeman Images: 41; Getty Images: Stock Montage, 24, Stringer/MPI, 20; Granger: 11 (top), 23, 27, 28, 32, 35, 43; Library of Congress: 16, 29; New York Public Library: cover (back); North Wind Picture Archives: 8, 13, 14, 18, 31, 36, 38; Pixabay: MIH83, background (throughout); Shutterstock: chrupka, 9, 12, 33, FashionStock.com, 45, Rido, cover (front), Sean Lema, 4; Wikimedia: Public Domain, 7, 11 (bottom)

All internet sites appearing in back matter were available and accurate when this book was sent to press.

Printed in the Unites States
PA117

Table of Contents

Words in **bold** are in the glossary.

Was the "New World" Really New?

WHAT WAS THE "NEW WORLD" LIKE?

When Europeans first traveled across the Atlantic Ocean, they found a beautiful new land. Thick forests, clear rivers, and blue skies were filled with wildlife of every kind. This was North America in the early 1500s. But Europeans were not the first people in the "New World." Many Native nations, such as the Wampanoag, Powhatan, and Roanoke people, already called this beautiful world their home. Each Native nation had its own lands, language, and **culture**. The Native people lived in harmony with nature.

When colonists arrived in North America they found a land filled with natural beauty.

WHAT WAS THE "OLD WORLD" LIKE?

Life was much different in the "Old World." More than 60 million people lived in Europe. Nobles owned most of the farmland, which was worked by poor peasants. Countries often fought bloody wars to gain power. To pay for them, leaders often taxed people heavily.

It wasn't long before the problems of the Old World spilled into the new. The riches of the New World would benefit many Europeans. But the Native people in America would have a very different experience.

What brought these two worlds together? And how did Europeans change the land and the lives of the Native people of North America?

Important Events in the Colonies

1492: Christopher Columbus reaches what will become the Americas

1587: Roanoke Island is settled by the English

1607: Jamestown, first permanent settlement, established by the English

1610: First of three Anglo-Powhatan Wars

1620: Pilgrims settle in Plymouth, Massachusetts

1630: Puritans form the Massachusetts Bay Colony

1682: Pennsylvania established by William Penn

1732: Georgia becomes the last of America's 13 colonies

1763: England creates boundary for its colonies called the Royal Proclamation

CHAPTER 1

Why Did Europeans Travel to America?

WHY DID EUROPEANS START EXPLORING THE WORLD?

Many events set the stage for the old and new worlds to meet. In the 1200s, Italian explorer Marco Polo traveled through Asia. He wrote about the valuable spices, silk, and jewels he saw on his trip. People in Europe, especially its rulers, were fascinated by his story.

Europe's leaders wanted the rich treasures of Asia for themselves. They also wanted a faster and easier way to reach them. Several explorers hoped to discover fast new routes to Asia. Some sailed south around Africa and then east to reach Asia by ship.

However, Christopher Columbus had another idea. The Italian explorer believed he could reach Asia by sailing west.

Christopher Columbus spotted the Bahama islands on October 12, 1492. He quickly landed on one and claimed it for Spain. However, the island wasn't empty. It was already home to the Taino people.

Columbus convinced Spanish royalty to pay for an **expedition**. In August 1492 Columbus sailed west with three ships: the *Niña*, the *Pinta*, and the *Santa María*. When he discovered land that October he thought he'd reached Asia. But he was wrong.

WHO FOLLOWED CHRISTOPHER COLUMBUS?

Once news of Columbus's **voyage** spread, other explorers followed. One was Amerigo Vespucci. He traveled westward and discovered Columbus's mistake. Columbus hadn't found Asia. He instead found a land unknown to Europeans. News quickly spread that there was another world to explore across the ocean.

Soon more explorers sailed west, including Ferdinand Magellan and Henry Hudson. Some found riches in the form of gold and silver. Most found huge areas of useful land. Although many Native nations already lived there, European leaders soon wanted to start colonies in the "New World."

Henry Hudson traded with several Native people while exploring the New World. The Hudson River was later named after him.

Routes of Early Explorers

— Amerigo Vespucci
— Christopher Columbus
— Ferdinand Magellan
— Henry Hudson

WHO WERE THE FIRST COLONISTS?

In 1584, England's Queen Elizabeth I gave Sir Walter Raleigh the right to settle in America. In 1585 he tried to start a colony on Roanoke Island in present-day North Carolina. But the settlers struggled with disease and lack of food. Violent conflicts with some of the Native nations there also made life very difficult. The colony failed.

King James I of England gave the Virginia and Plymouth Companies permission to form colonies in 1606. These companies provided the money and people to start the colonies. The king would rule over the people and the lands they settled.

CHAPTER 2

Why Did the English Settle in America?

WHAT WERE THE CHALLENGES OF LIFE IN ENGLAND?

Challenges in England made life hard for many people. England's population doubled between 1500 and 1650. There weren't enough jobs for everyone. This made it hard for people to survive. In the country, poor villagers got very small plots of land. But it wasn't enough for people to make a living from their crops. Many sold their land and left their villages hoping to find a better life.

WHAT DID THE "NEW WORLD" OFFER?

People willing to settle in America were promised land and opportunity. Many chose to take the risk of starting over in the New World. The first English settlers to travel to America settled on Roanoke Island in 1585. They were given 500 acres of land and the ability to take part in Roanoke's government.

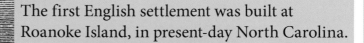

The first English settlement was built at Roanoke Island, in present-day North Carolina.

FACT

Sir Walter Raleigh said the purpose of settling in America was "To seek new worlds for gold, for praise, for glory."

Sir Walter Raleigh

WHAT CHALLENGES DID RELIGIOUS PEOPLE FACE IN ENGLAND?

Many people faced religious **persecution** in England. The country's national church was called the Church of England. Some people didn't agree with how it worked. They were forced to follow certain rules and traditions.

English Settlements and Colonies in North America

New Hampshire

New York

Massachusetts

Pennsylvania

Rhode Island

Connecticut

New Jersey

Delaware

Virginia

Maryland

North Carolina

South Carolina

Georgia

- 13 Colonies
- Jamestown Colony
- Massachusetts Bay Colony
- Plymouth Colony
- Roanoke Colony

Separatists

Some people wanted to form new churches and worship in their own way. They were called Separatists. At first it was illegal to be a Separatist. These people were considered **traitors**. Some were arrested because of their beliefs. Others lost their jobs and homes.

Quakers

Another religious group felt they should be able to worship without going to a church. They were called the Quakers. The Quakers believed God was present in everyone. They felt all people should be treated equally. And they worked to support groups that others mistreated. Many Quakers were also arrested for their beliefs. Some were even whipped and tortured.

The Quakers were known as the Religious Society of Friends. Many were arrested because they refused to swear an oath of loyalty to the English Crown.

DID PEOPLE FIND RELIGIOUS FREEDOM IN THE COLONIES?

Separatists came to America to find religious freedom. Two groups settled in Massachusetts. The Pilgrims settled in Plymouth. Meanwhile, the Puritans formed the Massachusetts Bay Colony. These two colonies later combined into one.

The Quakers also hoped to find a safe place to practice their beliefs. But many were persecuted in America too. Quakers were often killed by Puritans in Massachusetts.

Stories say William Penn met the Lenni Lenape nation under a large elm tree in present-day Philadelphia, Pennsylvania. It's thought that the two sides agreed to a treaty of peaceful friendship.

In 1682 a Quaker named William Penn formed Pennsylvania. The colony's purpose was to provide religious freedom. Many people moved from England to settle there.

David Zeisberger was a minister and missionary to the Lenape people during the mid-1700s.

Why Did Colonists Try to Spread Their Beliefs?

Some white Europeans believed that all people should be Christians. They tried to **convert** Native people to follow Christianity. They believed that Native people would have better lives as Christians and by living as farmers or in small settlements like they did.

But other colonists wanted to convert Native people so they could take the land for themselves. Some Europeans also saw Native people as being uncivilized. They wanted to **assimilate** Native people and remove them from their way of life. Over time, many Native nations lost not only their land, but also their language and culture.

CHAPTER 3

How Did Settlers' Lives Change in the Colonies?

Many settlers found great success after moving to the "New World." But others struggled to make a new life for themselves. They often faced problems they hadn't expected.

By signing the Mayflower Compact, the Pilgrims and other settlers agreed to work together to help the colony succeed.

DID SETTLERS ALWAYS AGREE WITH ONE ANOTHER?

Colonists had to work together to survive, but they often argued among themselves. When the Pilgrims came to North America, they traveled with another group of colonists on the *Mayflower*. But the two groups disagreed about where to build a settlement. They were supposed to land in an area controlled by the Virginia Company. But because of stormy seas, they landed in present-day Cape Cod, Massachusetts, instead.

In Virginia the Pilgrims would have had an official government and laws to follow. But they didn't have these things in Massachusetts. And the other colonists weren't sure if it was legal to settle where they had landed. The other settlers felt that they should leave. They wanted to start a separate settlement with its own government and laws. But the Pilgrims knew that would weaken both groups. They would be stronger together.

To solve this problem the colonists and Pilgrims wrote and signed the Mayflower Compact on November 11, 1620. This agreement formed a government and created laws that would benefit the whole colony.

WHAT WAS LIFE LIKE WHEN COLONISTS FIRST ARRIVED IN THE "NEW WORLD"?

Many settlers thought life would be better in America than in Europe. But they were in for a surprise. Building new settlements took a lot of hard work. And people often lived in difficult conditions until their new homes were built.

Colonists in Massachusetts struggled with cold, hunger, and disease during their first winter in 1620–1621.

The Pilgrims arrived at Plymouth Rock in Massachusetts in December 1620. Winter was just beginning, and there were no houses to live in. So the Pilgrims lived on the *Mayflower* while they built their settlement. This took several months. Their homes weren't ready until the following March. By then more than half of the Pilgrims had died.

Many of the Pilgrims died of disease. The long journey to America had weakened them and made them more likely to get sick. The poor living conditions after they arrived also helped to spread disease.

Some colonists fell ill with viruses they had brought to America. But others faced new illnesses. Many Jamestown settlers caught deadly diseases from mosquitoes and dirty water. With fewer people to build houses and grow food, it became harder for the colonists to survive.

FACT
Many settlers lost family members to hunger or disease in the colonies. One colonist in Virginia wrote, "... God be thanked I am now in good health, but my brother and my wife are dead about a year past."

DID THE COLONISTS HAVE ENOUGH FOOD?

Famine was also a problem in the colonies. Many settlers didn't know how to grow crops in America. The soil was different than in England. They needed to learn different farming methods and how to plant new crops.

When settlers first arrived in Jamestown, Virginia, in 1607, many were too busy searching for gold to do any work. They didn't bother to store food for winter or dig wells for fresh water.

In June 1610, the Jamestown settlers were ready to leave. But then Thomas West arrived with more people and supplies to save the colony.

The settlers struggled to survive for the next three years. Of the 500 Jamestown settlers, more than 400 died of hunger. In May 1610, Thomas Gates arrived with more colonists. Gates had been hired by the Virginia Company to be the new governor. But they had only brought a small supply of food. There wasn't enough for everyone. So in June, Gates decided they would all sail back to England.

However, as the colonists were leaving Chesapeake Bay, they were stopped by Thomas West. He had orders from the company to take control of the colony. He brought several ships with more settlers and plenty of supplies. He ordered the settlers to return to Jamestown. Living conditions there slowly improved. A colonist named John Rolfe started growing tobacco. The colony soon began selling it to England and earning a profit.

FACT

The settlers of Jamestown were so desperate for food, some even practiced **cannibalism**. One colonist wrote, ". . . nothing was spared to maintain life and to do those things which seem incredible, as to dig up dead corpse(s) out of graves and to eat them . . ."

CHAPTER 4

How Did Colonists and Native Nations Treat Each Other?

European settlers and people from the Native nations often didn't know how to react to each other. They often felt fearful or confused by each other's strange customs and appearance. Some were curious. Some were generous. But others were cruel. People's reactions often depended on their past experiences.

WHO WERE WANCHESE AND MANTEO?

English settlers first arrived at Roanoke Island in the spring of 1584. They spent two months trying to find a good place to build a settlement. They later returned to England to report their findings. Two Native people sailed back with them. One was Wanchese, ruler of the Roanoke nation. The other was Manteo, chief of the Croatoan people.

The first English explorers arrived at Roanoke Island in 1584. At first, the Native people there were nervous. But they soon became curious and friendly with white men.

Wanchese and Manteo learned how to speak English in Europe. They returned to Roanoke Island in 1585. But the two men had very different opinions of the English settlers. Wanchese went back to his people and told them that the colonists could not be trusted. Manteo, on the other hand, supported them. Over the next year, the settlers had several conflicts with the Roanoke nation. Meanwhile, they had friendly relations with the Croatoans.

In 1590 John White discovered that the Roanoke settlement was empty. The settlers' fate remains a mystery to this day.

WHAT HAPPENED AT THE ROANOKE COLONY?

The first settlement on Roanoke Island didn't last. The colonists suffered through a rough winter, food shortages, and disease. In the summer of 1586, the surviving settlers returned to England. Fifteen soldiers stayed behind to guard the land until more colonists could arrive with supplies. In 1587 Governor John White arrived at Roanoke Island with 100 settlers. But the soldiers that had been left behind were gone.

Manteo told White that Wanchese's people had killed the English soldiers. He helped White plan an attack on the Roanoke people at night. But the English didn't realize that the Roanoke had left the area. They accidentally killed several Croatoan people instead.

That fall John White returned to England for more supplies. But a war with Spain kept him from returning for three years. When he finally did return in 1590, the settlers were all gone. The only clue he found was the word "CROATOAN" carved into a wooden post.

White believed the settlers had moved to live with the Croatoan people on a nearby island. But fierce storms prevented him from sailing there to find out. White eventually had to return to England. The settlers of Roanoke Island were never seen or heard from again.

WHAT CAUSED CONFLICT BETWEEN THE JAMESTOWN COLONY AND THE POWHATAN NATION?

The Jamestown settlement was built near the Powhatan nation. The Powhatan people traded food with the colonists for tools and other goods. The English settlers spent a lot of time looking for gold. They didn't grow or store much food for winter. So they soon became dependent on the Powhatan for food.

However, Jamestown's leader, Captain John Smith, didn't trust in the Powhatan's kindness. He decided to steal what the colony needed instead. He destroyed Powhatan villages and took their food by force. These actions were the beginning of the First Anglo-Powhatan War. Chief Powhatan told his people to stop trading with the English and attack them instead.

Chief Powhatan also captured and kept some of the English as prisoners. In response, the colonists took the chief's daughter, Pocahontas. To get her back, they demanded the return of their men and a supply of tools and weapons.

Chief Powhatan returned the prisoners, but refused to give any tools or weapons. The English kept Pocahontas prisoner for a year. During that time she converted to Christianity. She later married colonist John Rolfe in 1614. They travelled to England in 1616, but Pocahontas died on the return trip to Virginia in 1617.

The marriage of Pocahontas to John Rolfe helped bring peace between the colonists and the Powhatan people for the next several years.

HOW DID SQUANTO HELP THE PILGRIMS?

Many Pilgrims died from hunger and disease during their first winter in Plymouth. But in the spring of 1621, they met Squanto from the Pawtuxet nation. He spoke English and taught them how to fish and plant crops such as corn. He showed them how to get sap from maple trees. He taught them which plants were poisonous and which were safe to eat. Squanto also helped the Pilgrims communicate with people in the Wampanoag nation.

Squanto was friendly toward the Pilgrims. He showed them how to grow and gather food for their settlement.

The first Thanksgiving took place in 1621. It was a friendly celebration between the Pilgrims and the Wampanoag people.

That November the Pilgrims shared a feast with the Wampanoag after their first harvest. This peaceful celebration between English settlers and Native nations became known as the first Thanksgiving.

How do Native people feel about Thanksgiving?

Today many Native people have mixed feelings about Thanksgiving. Some like to think about the things they are thankful for. But others get upset by the **stereotypes** the holiday creates. History books often describe Native nations inaccurately, and their true customs have been forgotten. Some Native people consider Thanksgiving to be a day of mourning. Although the Wampanoag people and Pilgrims got along, many other Native nations were hurt by the colonists.

HOW DID SQUANTO LEARN TO SPEAK ENGLISH?

Squanto's ability to speak English proved useful to the Pilgrims. However, this skill came at a cost. He had learned the language after being kidnapped by an Englishman and sold into slavery. Years later, Squanto escaped and returned to America. He later learned that his Pawtuxet people had died of disease.

Squanto joined the Wampanoag nation and became an **interpreter** for the English settlers. Few Native people knew how to speak English. Squanto knew he was in a rare position. He used his abilities to gain power over other Native people. For example, he told them that if they didn't do what he asked, he would get the English to release a deadly plague.

FACT

The Pilgrims were wary of Native people at first. The Pilgrims didn't want them to know how many settlers had died during their first winter. They hid the truth by flattening their burial ground and planting grain upon it.

Squanto was kidnapped and sold into slavery in Spain in 1614.

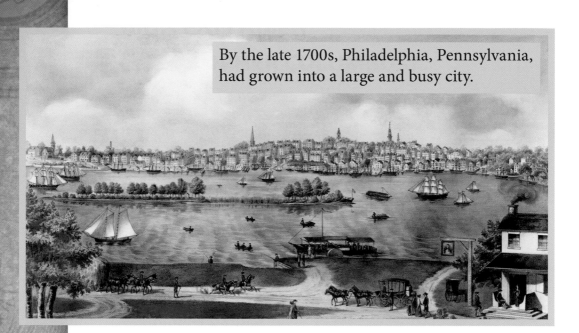

By the late 1700s, Philadelphia, Pennsylvania, had grown into a large and busy city.

WHAT HAPPENED WHEN THE COLONIES CONTINUED TO GROW?

England knew the lands in the "New World" belonged to the Native nations. But they built more colonies anyway. Soon there were 13 in all. These included Connecticut, Delaware, Georgia, Maryland, Massachusetts, New Jersey, New Hampshire, New York, North Carolina, Pennsylvania, Rhode Island, South Carolina, and Virginia.

In 1763 England issued a Royal Proclamation. It stated that colonists would not settle in lands beyond the Applachian Mountains. A Creek chief called this boundary ". . . a stone wall never to be broke."

But the English colonists didn't keep their word. By 1770 more than 2 million people lived in the 13 colonies. This included European colonists and enslaved black people. More room was needed. The English began taking more land for their colonies. They expanded beyond the boundaries they had agreed to just a few years before. With less land and fewer resources, life grew more difficult for the Native people.

Royal Proclamation Border, 1763

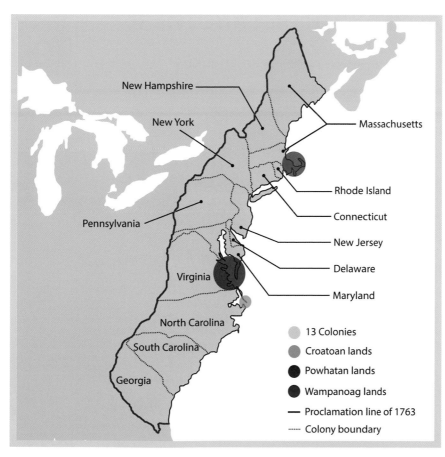

New Hampshire

New York

Massachusetts

Rhode Island

Connecticut

New Jersey

Delaware

Pennsylvania

Maryland

Virginia

North Carolina

South Carolina

Georgia

- 13 Colonies
- Croatoan lands
- Powhatan lands
- Wampanoag lands
— Proclamation line of 1763
······ Colony boundary

CHAPTER 5

How Did Life Change for Native People?

The lives of Native people changed a great deal when English colonists settled in America. Unfortunately, most of the changes made their lives more difficult.

DID NATIVE NATIONS ALWAYS AGREE WITH ONE ANOTHER?

When settlers came to the New World, it created many problems for the Native nations. But Native people had different views on what to do about those problems. This led to conflict between various Native nations.

After settlers came to Roanoke Island, several events took place. When the first group of settlers left there was a total **eclipse** of the sun. And when they returned, a comet was seen in the night sky. Many Native people then died from a deadly disease.

Hundreds of years ago, some Native people thought solar eclipses, comets, and similar events were signs that bad times were ahead.

Several Roanoke people thought these were bad signs. They thought the English brought only death and hardship. But they disagreed about what to do about it. Some wanted to be friendly to the English. Meanwhile, others wanted to avoid the settlers at all costs. The disagreements eventually led to violent conflicts and the death of the Roanoke chief, Wingina.

The Native nations had no resistance to diseases brought by the colonists. Tens of thousands of Native people suffered and died from smallpox, measles, flu, and other deadly diseases.

HOW WERE NATIVE NATIONS AFFECTED BY DISEASE?

The colonists carried many deadly diseases with them from Europe. Some of these included smallpox, measles, and influenza. People in the Native nations had no **immunity** to these diseases. They had never been sick with them before.

European diseases spread and worsened quickly among Native people. One explorer wrote, "Within a few days after our departure from every such [Indian] town, the people began to die very fast . . . in some towns about twenty, in some forty, in some sixty . . . The disease was also so strange that they neither knew what it was nor how to cure it."

It's believed that 80 to 90 percent of Native people died from deadly European diseases. Experts think that Native people might have defeated the Jamestown colony if they hadn't been weakened by the diseases they suffered.

FACT
Some settlers might have tried to make Native people sick on purpose. In 1763 Sir Jeffery Amherst, a commander in the British Army, suggested sending blankets infected with smallpox to Native people in Pennsylvania. A short time later, many Native people became sick with smallpox. But it's unknown if the deadly disease was spread by the blankets or something else.

?

Most Native people understood that nature provided for their needs. They respected the land and tried to live in peace with nature.

HOW WERE NATIVE PEOPLE'S BELIEFS AND CULTURE AFFECTED?

Most Native nations had different beliefs about the land than the colonists. The English believed that land should be taken and used for profit. But many Native people, including the Powhatan, Roanoke, and Wampanoag, believed that the land should be respected. They felt that it couldn't be owned or sold by any one person. Instead, it was meant to be shared by all living things.

Many settlers wanted the Native nations to change their views. They wanted Native people to assimilate with European culture and beliefs. The colonists often considered them to be "savages." Settlers often thought it was their job to "civilize" Native people and turn them into what they considered "proper, upstanding people."

To achieve this goal, colonists often tried to get Native people to give up their cultures. They wanted Native people to live more like Europeans, to speak English, and wear European clothes.

CHAPTER 6

How Did the Colonies Change America?

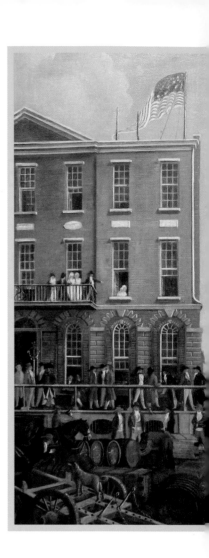

After years of hard work and struggle, English colonists could finally call America home. The colonies were filled with busy towns and cities. Farms were filled with crops and livestock. The freedoms and opportunities in the New World gave settlers more abundant and fulfilling lives.

But what effect did the colonists have on the land? How did they change North America's beautiful forests and natural wetlands? What happened to the animals and birds that once thrived in the colonies? And how did life change for the Native nations who already called this place home?

By the 1700s, the colonies were thriving. Cities like New York and Philadelphia were filled with people from Europe and around the world.

FACT

Experts believe 900,000 to 18 million Native people lived in the Americas before Europeans arrived. The Native nations spoke up to 500 different languages. But by 1880, only about 300,000 Native people lived in North America.

WHAT CHANGES WERE MADE TO THE NEW WORLD?

The settlers had built a new life in the colonies. But their presence caused drastic changes. Many of America's forests were cut down. Instead of lands full of trees and wildlife, much of it became flat farmland.

Settlers also brought diseases from Europe that destroyed many Native nations. The surviving Native people were then forced to live in a strange, new world. This was just the beginning. Before long, settlers began pushing farther west. Eventually they pushed out Native nations across the continent and claimed their lands for themselves. It's hard to imagine how America changed so much in a fairly short time. But it did.

By the middle 1700s, much of America's large forests had been flattened and turned into farmland.

Today the United States is one of the richest and most powerful countries in the world. But people need to ask the question: Was it worth the cost? Was creating a new nation worth the drastic changes to the land? Could the colonists have settled in America and preserved the lives and cultures of Native people? You'll have to decide for yourself.

More Questions About the American Colonies

Who were the most important people during the settlement of America?

- Queen Elizabeth I was the ruler of England in the late 1500s. She granted Sir Walter Raleigh permission to form a settlement on Roanoke Island. She hoped it would help England in its war against Spain.

- Squanto was a Native of the Pawtuxet nation who helped the Pilgrims survive. He was also called Tisquantum.

- Pocahontas was the daughter of Chief Powhatan. According to one story, colonist John Smith was about to be killed by a Powhatan warrior. But Pocahontas ran to his side and prevented the attack. Historians aren't sure the story is true. Some say that Smith might have made the whole story up.

- John Rolfe helped Jamestown prosper by planting and growing tobacco. His marriage to Pocahontas helped bring peace between the settlers and the Powhatan people.

Who settled the rest of North and South America?

- Canada was mostly settled by France. The French had positive relationships with many Native nations and traded with them for animal furs.

- Mexico, Central America, and South America were mostly settled by Spain. The Spanish often treated Native people poorly by enslaving or killing them.

GLOSSARY

assimilate (uh-SIM-uh-layt)—to become familiar with and fit in to the culture of another population or group

cannibalism (KA-nuh-buhl-ism)—the practice of eating the flesh of another person

convert (kuhn-VURT)—to change from one religion or faith to another

culture (KUHL-chur)—the way of life, ideas, beliefs, art, and traditions of a group of people

eclipse (i-KLIPS)—an event in which the moon's shadow passes over the earth

expedition (ek-spuh-DI-shuhn)—a journey with a goal, such as exploring or searching for something

famine (FA-muhn)—a serious shortage of food resulting in widespread hunger and death

immunity (ih-MYOO-ni-tee)—the ability of the body to resist disease

interpreter (in-TUR-prit-uhr)—a person who translates what is said in one language to another language to help people understand each other

persecution (pur-si-KYOO-shuhn)—cruel or unfair treatment, often because of race or religious beliefs

stereotype (STER-ee-oh-tipe)—an exaggerated and often inaccurate idea or description of a person, group, or thing

traitor (TRAY-tuhr)—someone who betrays his or her country or beliefs

voyage (VOI-ij)—a long journey to a distant place, usually in a ship

READ MORE

Loh-Hagan, Virginia. *Roanoke Colony.* Ann Arbor, MI: 45th Parallel Press, 2018.

McAneney, Caitie. *Uncovering the Jamestown Colony.* New York: Gareth Stevens Publishing, 2017.

Micklos Jr, John. *Explorers and American Indians.* North Mankato, MN: Capstone Press, 2017.

INTERNET SITES

British America: Thirteen Colonies
https://www.dkfindout.com/us/history/american-revolution/british-america-thirteen-colonies/

The First Thanksgiving
https://kids.nationalgeographic.com/explore/history/first-thanksgiving/

The Pilgrims and Plymouth Colony
https://www.ducksters.com/history/colonial_america/pilgrims_plymouth_colony.php

INDEX